TWO EAGLES

TWO EAGLES

Rudy H. Garcia

Red Engine Press
Fort Smith, Arkansas

Copyright © 2025 Rudy H. Garcia

ALL RIGHTS RESERVED. No part of this book may be reproduced or transmitted in any form or by any means, electronic or mechanical, including photocopying, recording, or by any information storage and retrieval system (except by a reviewer or commentator who may quote brief passages in a printed or on-line review) without permission of the publisher.

Cover art by Risa E. Garcia

Library of Congress Control Number: 2025933102

ISBN: 979-8-9895620-8-4 (softcover)

2nd Printing

Dedication

Two Eagles is dedicated to my lovely wife Rita, our darling daughters Risa, Mari, Marisa & Carisa, our precious Grandchildren and to all the Two Eagles children of America.

Contents

1 — Childhood Memories 1
2 — Immigration Matters 35
3 — Schools & Education 87
4 — Hope ❤ Faith ❤ Love 119
About the Author 147

1 – Childhood Memories

Two Eagles

Two Majestic Eagles Soar Great Heights for Thee.
Constant symbols,
That thy SPIRIT is Free.
What Miraculous Evolutionary Consequence,
To have
Not one
But two
High Flying Emblems
Impressed Forever
Upon Thy Chest.
What Great Distinction,
Grace's Thee,
To have
Two
Sky Kings
Soar for Thee.

Mamas Said

It was not so long ago,
When taking tacos for lunch
To school, wasn't cool.

It was humiliating, embarrassing
And even dog-gone degrading,
For a mere handful of kids
To decide school lunch standards.

That peanut butter and jelly,
Should be the food to fill your hungry belly,
And being snickered at, because of our folded taco
And its bean-papas, tortilla filling
Was not at all a good feeling.

Mamas felt that embarrassing feeling too,
After all, Mamas know you know,
They know when their child is hurting.

It's like some sort of mystical maternal radar instinct
They imbed in us, during our fetal development.
Forging an uninterruptable bond with each passing trimester
And continuing to strengthen after our birthing.

So, to avoid that teasing lunch time trauma,
When Pandora's deeds were released
From Roy Rogers, Trigger's and Barbie lunch boxes.

Mamas said,
We come home for lunch instead.

No cold box lunch for us, mamas said.
Mamas said…
You'll come home for hot *sopita,*
Just like your dad… our mamas said.

And so, it was… every day… right at high noon,
When the school lunch bell rang,
We, *todo Mundo*, practically flew,
To our Mamas' *cocina,*
Leaving behind us
Only those few.

And us? Well, we us… *sabrosisimo*, slurped down,
Two steaming, full *platos tupidos de sopa.*

Papas con pacadillo, on Monday,
Fideo con pollo, Tuesday,
Conchitas con carne, Wednesday,
Arroz con pollo, Thursday,
And always, *pescado frito,* on Friday.
We're Catholic so we never eat meat on Friday.

And ever and always,
A tall stack of fresh
Just off the smoking Comal.
Aromatic tortillas,
Sometimes flour,
Sometimes corn,
And yes!
O' my God!
Sometimes *gorditas de manteca!*

Iced tea, some days, sweet *limonada* other days and
sometimes green, or yellow, red or purple cool-aide to
drink.

Other weekdays, depending on the season,
We had,
Calabacita con pollo or *calabacita con puerco*,
Or *macaron con carne*
And *nopalitos*, with you name it during the Lenten season.

During winter, months,
Still, we walked home for lunch at noon.
The menu consisted of soups… *Caldo de pollo* or *Caldo de res*,
And of course, every Friday, quite often,
Caldo de pes.

Mamas knew,
That a meal, any meal,
Was not complete
Unless served with beans.
Pinto beans,
Frijoles pintos,

Refritos, almost all the time,
Charra, sometimes,
En bola other times.

For years and years,
Twelve years in fact.
We never ate lunch at school.
For us,
It wasn't cool.

You had to be some kind of stupid fool,
To pass up Mama's lunch
And take your lunch to school.

No, it was not that long ago,
When the entire barrio,
Went home for lunch instead
Because that's what Mamas said.

Miss Rodriguez

She had the most beautiful tender hands,
Soft and smooth, like cotton tail bunny fur.
Always aromatic, with jasmine, gardenia scented Jergens
hand crème lotion.

Her slender fingers… straight and flawless.
They didn't show a diamond ring,
Nor vows beholding wedding band, she wore no type of
ring at all.

She kept them neat and manicured,
With shinny polish, bright no smears.
And when she taught, she sang with them, like Gauguin's
girls, to whom he ran.

She didn't keep those nails too long,
Yet long enough to make you think.
And never used the polish red, she always kept them
pretty in pink.

I used the youthful mischief ploy,
Of a foolish growing boy,
In her morning, English class,
To roust her beauty over to me, over by my carved-up
desk.

I did all this to misbehave.
For her to punish me,
For her to pinch me,
With her enchanting fingernails, hoping she would tip the scales.

She was my tenth-grade language arts teacher.
Miss Rodriguez was her name.
She always dressed so fine, so very classy, matching shoes, to purse, to dress, never messy.

Her lips were perfect… made for kissing.
Lips, like hers I'd never seen.
They weren't, like skinny chicken lips,
They weren't no dried-up wafer lips, they were Diana Ross's swollen lips,

They were the perfect kissing lips.
They were inviting, rosy lips.
And to no one yet, she gave a taste, at least, that's what she always said.

Said I, to her, dear darling, my "La Miss",
Please, please, please, do please, let me…
Please, dare not, let those lovely lips go to waste! Let me, let me, all I ask is a iddy-biddy taste!

You silly boy, she said to me,
But you're so funny, and not even a tiny bit, coy.
Behave yourself, just do your lessons, you and me, it cannot be.

Her hair was brilliant, raven jet,
Perfumed with fresh smelling
New rain shampoo.
She styled like Mary Tyler Moore
And bounced my feelings to the core.
She kinda, even walked like her, like smiling, Mary Tyler Moore,
My Miss Rodriguez did this and more.

Her skin was tanner than suntan.
A very dark brown, angel tan.
Inherited from Africa's Kings, who married into Aztec Queens.

It wasn't black
It wasn't light
It was brown royal, smooth, very swarthy,
Silky as the deep, purple, starry, starry, Milky Way, night…

Ms. Boudreaux

She had traveled the world; a world traveler was she,
With many acquired customs and cultured languages.
Her father, was a civil engineer, bridge builder,
Industrial and commercial, canal waterway digger,
With accomplished jobs, all around the globe.
She showed us pictures of the Panama Canal,
The Suez Canal, the Erie Canal and the
Intercostal waterways, from Texas to Florida.

Miss Boudreaux was her name, Diane.
She came to us during our seventh-grade school year.
Measuring at about five foot three, one hundred ten pounds.
A beautiful, brand new excited schoolteacher,
With "I love Lucy" hair and unconditional kindness.

Pretty legs, very pretty, not too skinny legs, not to skinny at all,
Not too chubby, not chubby, very shapely, very shapely.
She had amber freckles, coating her radiant cover girl face.
Slightly golden, kinda, sunset-golden, light brown-reddish,
Thousands and thousands of freckles…
And when we made her angry, those freckles turned a blazing neon red.
She had them all over her entire lily-white body.
And her eyes were a singing pastel blue.

She taught us English; she taught us Spanish,
She also taught us, the fancy foreign language, French.
Par-le-vou-fran-say, nes- pa, sene- pa- grraaave,
We-we- mo-na-mí,
Joe- no-say-qua, and *se quito el carzon.*
She transformed us… a Mexiquito, Chicanito, rowdy bunch…
Mono-lingual, Spanish mostly, English sometimes,
Into a multi-lingual speaking, refreshingly enriched,
enlightened group…

It was 1967–68… LBJ… and his Great Society…
And the women lib girls of the rocking-rolling sixties.
All used their skirts and dresses above the knee,
Polyester came to be, hippies, flower power,
And love was free.
They called them mini dresses
Some wore them three inches above the knees, some wore them
Four or more inches above, they called those maxis.
Miss Boudreaux, with great delight and fantasizes,
To us pubic sprouting boys,
Wore her dresses right at four
Inches, above her praying knees.
Yes, I remember very clearly
She was the picture-perfect, size four.

The Switch

O' Scarlet Stripes,
O' Purple Stripes,
O' Black and Blue Embedded Stripes.

The Switch!
It Stings!
It Rips!
It Welts on me!

It prejudicially imprints itself,
On tiny hands and little arms,
On small Children's legs for all to see,

Resulting insult, of that Racist decree,
Inflicting punishment
For speaking Spanish in public,
School grounds, of a free country.

Nothing Sad

And so, we parted ways, I to the university,
You to live in the city.
Friends forever we said.
Let's write to each other… nothing sad.

Perhaps, during Christmas holiday we can meet,
Share a meal at Isabel's café, on Canal Street.
You can tell me how you are doing,
And I will tell you how I am doing.

Nothing Sad….

Viejo Storyteller Jacinto

Viejo tells us the story.
Tell us the story about
Jacinto Treviño.
Tell us what happened back then
In 1910, between Jacinto Treviño
And the *Rinche* Texas Rangers.
Tell us again how Jacinto,
Sent all the Rangers running,
With their tail between their legs,
Scurrying and yapping like crying dogs,
Looking for a place to hide
Out of Jacinto's way.
Tell us, how Jacinto, would be rolling on the ground,
Tickling all over with laughter at such a sight,
Rinches running cowardly,
Scattered, practically flying, eyes wide open with fright
And mouths gasping for what they believed
Could be their last intake of life's air.

Tell, Viejito, of the three separate times,
When Jacinto, cursed, the *Rinches* Rangers
And lived to tell about it
In his old age,
You tell it so clear,
As if it happened just yesterday,
With twinkling eyes
And a satisfied smile

Tell us ancient crier,
Of those days long ago.
When being born Mexican in Texas,
Meant being born deformed,

With your head tilted downward,
Eyes to the ground,
Sunken chest, shoulders bent, small brain,
Small enough to understand
And conform to his even smaller position
In Texas.
Small enough to understand
That his life didn't matter.
To be imposed,
To be disposed,
To be whatever patron supposed,
Was good enough for him.

Tell us O' Viejo historian,
Of those days back then
When Jacinto Treviño,
Challenged the *Rinche* Rangers
To a duel in Brownsville, Texas.
And how the Rangers ran
At that figure's sight.
A tall standing Mexican,
Well dressed, well-armed.
His ten-gallon hat,
Tilted slightly,
On his straightforward looking head
And not in his hands,
As was the custom back then,
If Mexican addressing a "white."
To see a Mexican in Texas,
Standing at full alert,
Pigeon chest, smiling proud,
Ready to draw his side arm.
To kill and be killed,
Was out of this world in 1910 Texas,
Unnatural, in fact.

Tell us dear Viejo *testigo*,
How Jacinto Treviño
And the *Rinche* Rangers
Had it out.
With guns, fists, kicks, bites,
Broken bottles, furniture and
Rinches, flying in all different directions.
Tell us how Jacinto
Kicked *Rinche* butt,
Not once, not twice, but three times,
Once in McAllen,
Once in Brownsville, and
Once in San Benito, Texas.

Tell us how never before
In the history of mankind.
A Mexican single-handedly
All by himself
Stood up and defeated
The Texas Rangers.
Gregorio Cortez, from Karnes City, Texas,
Gave them one hell of a run,
Until they jailed his wife and family.
Juan N. Cortina, took Brownsville, from them
But gave it back,
After both Mexico and Texas ganged up on him.
Catarino Garza, caused them
Lots of problems.
But never, no one, except
Jacinto Treviño, by himself
Kicked the Ranger's ass,
And lived to laugh and sing about it
Way into his golden years,
As he willfully waited for the *Rinche's* return to
Brownsville, Matamoros,

To execute his arrest.
But it never happened.
Because the *Rinches covardes*
Knew that they were
Facing a man.
The man, was, Jacinto Treviño.

Tell it again Viejo!

Vaquero-Cowboy

He scaffolds to his favorite bar stool and mounts,
Just like any other bow legged eighty-year-old Vaquero-Cowboy would.
Shifting his sweat ringed Stetson back on his head,
Exposing the burrowed, weathered and leathered canyons
Of raw-hide flesh, on his sun-roasted face.

He grins at the lovely *señorita*,
Working behind the bar
Lifting a broken, bent, sand-papered, calloused index,
He says,
Una fría por favor hijita,
As he pulls out a vintage, faded bandana…

He wipes at too many
Cattle round-ups to remember.
Too many, broken-bronco-bones, ago.
Too many rusted out, melted out, branding irons
And too many rode out, cast off, King Ranch saddles past.

He snaps the smoky, beer and whiskey stanched, cantina air,
With his ancient, pleaded cloth,
Capturing within its open range woven fabric,
All the echoing ghost voices, noises, and cattle driven faces
That once sat at that very same place.

He wipes his rugged brow then tucks the historical *pañuelo*,
Away, into his back discolored canvas Levi pocket.
Leaving a pointed corner hanging out,
Peering and absorbing anything else that happens by.
He raises his cold sweated, pilsner, foam-crested mug
To the beautiful *señorita*, Margarita tending bar.

SALUD… CHULITA!

Sailor

His creaking body, broken, maimed,
Shuffles to the water's edge.
Hunched and bent and foggy eyed,
He takes the eastern sun,
He's lame.

He lives with memories of Mariner days,
Of Ports O' Call, sea treasures hauled
And Maidens, longing for his loving ways.

He breathes, he tastes, the salty mist,
Reminder of what used to be.
An eager lad, and then a Captain
And all the angry waves he kissed.

Slowly raising a weathered hand,
His sailor cap he removes,
And thinks some more of days of yore,
He's moored now to the land.

With lots of pain and effort, too,
He stiffens, standing tall,
To face the currents of his love,
Lamenting the invitation of her call.

A kerchief, to the eye he plies,
As she dances, sings and waves on by.
Can he be sad? Or is he glad?
Or thinking, my, how time flies bye.

His back is to the western sun.
His shadow to the shore.
He waits to greet the moon once more,
Recalling sailing times before.

He wonders as he shuffles back,
Away from water's edge.
Will life tomorrow give him slack?
Or fail him thus to olden age?

No matter what the next day brings,
There's something, sure for sure.
He turns to her ... he says to her. "I may be beat...
But you come lapping at my feet."

Barge Pilot

Navy sailor WWII
Landing barge pilot
This ode is for you.

Never wavering against the monstrous, soulless, reaping, tempest,
Scything towards you, as an incarnated weapon from the other side of the earth.

Steaming, full open throttle, you charge the hostile beach carpeted with corpse red,
The preferential red-carpet treatment of war.

Your shell-shocked barge, drops its battled jaw at such homicidal reception
And out of its mouth, spews, languishing, dreadful pleads for absolution.

Boys made men…
Yell, scream, and cry out, No! Not yet! Not now! Don't send me out there just yet!

But fate prevails and Marines!
Not recruits, splash unto the deadly shore amidst a deluge of life siphoning, ripping bullets.

And you… you landing barge pilot, Captain of your boat, your soul,
Scream to every angel you can muster.

Get them off my deck!
Take these freshly initiated leathernecks off this floating iron casket!

Carry these liberators
And cast them unto that wrinkled, pleated, crimson carpet woven U.S.A. tight, with mangled arms and legs.

Then with empty hull, full throttle in reverse but never retreating!
Never turning your back on the enemy, you bayonet the foam crested breakers, splitting them with grit and rage.

Back to the mother ship, to reload your barge, to re-cock yourself, with nameless, faceless warriors.
You do not look to see their faces, what for?

You do not see a color, it's all a blur, you do not know a single seaman's name
It doesn't matter.

All that matters, is your transport, your delivery, to the fight, to the kill!
But not surrendering to death! Because from killing returns life!

Back and forth, back and forth, killing and killing, death and more death!
Killing for the sake of living!

Ship loads of mother's sons of liberty!
Disembarked armed, fighting missionaries of freedom, human wonders take the beach.

Mission completed…
Until, an untranquil silence permeates the warring burnt powdered air.

Finally,
The only sound you hear, is the morbid, idle, sputtering exhausted exhaust of your barge's expended motor.

Huddled, fawning, suckling, next to your ship's bosom,
You raise your blood curled eyes to her and wait… she sends down nothing.

Realizing that she has nothing else to give, nothing else to send and die
The combat battle is over.

Wearied, you do not turn to look to shore, no part of you returns there ever more
No part of you can, you left it all on the blood-soaked sand, there on foreign land.

Every piece of you…
Was taken by every Marine that plunged into the swallow shoal with the bottomless pit for the dead.

Exasperated and fatigued you curse away moribundity!
Sepulchering the horror, the explosive, the obtrusive,
Nightmarish noise of battle to the profoundness depth of your mind's abyss.
Hero!
You decommission your barge and march on solid ground, carpeted for you with parade and ticker tape.

The biggest public promenade you've ever seen, lined by
nameless, cheering, waving, grateful civilians.
Red, White and Blue pride engulfs you.

Sparkling, jingling medal and ribbon citations,
Adorn your robust, expanded chest. The war is ended and
you`re the Victor!

And on your Herculean, upper arm…Tattooed,
An Eagle, magnificently perched upon a cactus, wings
extended mightily.

A snake, dangles from its beak, a symbol of strength and
patriotism.
Your Badge of Courage.

Do you know a Shrimper?

Have you ever looked into the eyes of a weathered old shrimper?
Have you ever touched his monstrous, callous hands?
Have you ever noticed his tired shoulders once broad.
His crab claw like powerful arms, tattooed and scarred.

Have you noticed that his sea worn face is unlike yours and mine?
Have you ever wondered why he continually ventures back out to sea?
Have you ever prayed that he returns from there safe and sound?
Have you ever been there on the mooring docks, to welcome him home?

On Board a Shrimp Boat

Have you ever been aboard a shrimping boat?
With the Captain and his mates.
Have you ever held a deep-sea trawling net?
And wondered how the shrimp get in?
Or have you ever pulled a heavy sea soaked cabo rope?
That carves and measures the fathoms deep.

Have you ever paced a shrimp boat's slippery deck?
Or stood by anchor's prow,
Have you ever had an angry wave?
Slap you mercilessly across the face?
Have you ever climbed the towering mainmast?
During bitter cold winters or tropic tempest storms.

Have you ever fallen overboard, way far, too far from shore?
Never seen nor heard of again, never to be held again,
Never to be hugged again, never, never, more.
Have you ever, ever, been the one, the one with endless love?
The patient father/rosary beads praying mother … who lost a son at sea.

Have you ever been the loving wife, to kiss his lips no more?
Have you ever been the admiring child who lost a dad at sea?
Have you ever known a Shrimping man who lost his life at sea?

Many Days Out at Sea

Have you ever been too long, too many days away at sea?
And missed your newborn baby's birth,
His very first gay filled mirth,
Or when he climbed his first tall tree?
Were you around to even, see?
And hear him say, look dad… dad look at me!
Have you ever been too far out at sea?
Away from children's glee,
Too far to hear that blissful sound,
Unable to stroke their shiny crown,
Too far to comfort the weeping child,
And wipe away a pouting frown
Or tuck away your babe's goodnight,
Then morrow keep them within your constant sight.

Have you ever toiled too long at sea?

Have you ever spent too many days and nights of yesterday?
Trawling for shrimp, then washing riggings packed with oceans' bottom clay,
Mending nets, constantly coiling ropes, charting the course for the next sailing day,
Thirty – forty – fifty – sixty days, sailed out in March, docking back sometime in May.

Have you ever scrubbed and scrubbed and rubbed, then washed, shampooed your briny body?
From the embedded- penetrated, under your skin smell of the salty sea?

Of slimy netted shrimp gunk, of choking black bellowing exhaust diesel fuel fumes,
Or rusted iron from your hands, of slippery by-catch, staining your white rubber deck boots
Have you ever smelled a shrimper man who toiled too long at sea?

Have you ever been so long at sea?
To never hear your son's first A, B, C,
Your daughter's first count of one, two, three…
Not there to see them off for their first day of school
Or tell them both about the guiding golden rule
Or how the sea is composed of countless globules upon tiny globules.

Have you ever stayed that long at sea?

Navigators

Three and four wide, side by side,
Shrimp boats, sadistically hogtied, roped, and bonded together,
Languishing, moored, to rust away and decay, without a crew.

Rusty red pained stains and apathy streaking down
Both sides of a sea weathered cabin wheelhouse and pounded hull.

Unlike, what the Crown of thorns once did…

Line, after line, after line
Of loneliness, of solitude, of abandonment, zero hands on deck,
Forged by the senseless, unforgiving curse of bankruptcy,

Repositions, liens, oceans deep debts and deeper than oceans government regulations Trespass the heavy heart.

Of
Webbed and netted, tangled and bewildered mariners, who were once mighty, robust, thick, boosting, boisterous men.

Now, these once adventurous navigators of the seven seas, who once shone a bright powerful spotlight at other "passing ships in the night,"

Are now reduced to shining handheld flashlights,
Walking the night away pulling on commercial building`s doors
As security- guard- night, watchmen.

Used to Be

There walks another,
Mighty Shrimper, used to be.
The price of oil finished him.

There lies another,
Beached, driftwood, shrimp boat, used to be
Throw it on the bonfire.

Yell

One dollar a day
And all the sweet watermelon you can eat.

That sounds like a juicy deal
If you ask me.

I am asking you... replied
The *Sandiero gordo*, watermelon man.

What do I have to do for that dollar?
And all the watermelon I can eat.

You ride on the back of my pickup,
As we drive slowly through the barrio streets

And yell as loud as you can.
Yell, loud enough for all to hear.

Yell? But what will I yell?
Que te pasa muchacho, haven't you ever sold Sandias before?

No *señor*, I never have.
But, I sure can yell, I've yelled many, many times before. I can sure do that.

Bueno, entonces, this is what you are going to yell.
Sandia Barata, Sandia Barata, Sandia Barata

Sandia Barata?
Is that all I have to yell?

Si,
That's all.

Can I ask you a question Mr. Watermelon seller man…?
Yes, of course, but ask it pronto, gotta go, gotta sell.
What about, if I yell out loud,
Sandia Barata, Sandia Barata verde por afuera, colorada por adentro.

Good! Very good *muchacho*, that sounds very good!
You, Yell, *Sandia Barata, verde por afuera, colorada por adentro.*
And young man; someday, you to, might grow-up to be a *Sandiero,*
Watermelon man, just like me.

2 – Immigration Matters

I Listen to the River

I listen to the river,
Because my body is molded with its fertile clay.
My blood mingles with its rejuvenating water,
Cleansing my spirit free.

I listen to the river,
Because I hear over and over from the Eagle and the Jaguar,
That the name is *El Rio Bravo*…The Brave River,
I, too, am brave.

I listen to the river,
Because its currents, sing storied corridors, *corriendo* through me.
It sings to me in olden tongues, flowing mystically within me.
I hear the ancient melody of
Teco's verses fishing for bass, Navajo maidens chanting, washing, by its shallow banks, Comanche yelps, watering painted ponies.
And La Llorona's eternal, repenting, sorrowful woes, searching,
For the bodies of her starving Angelinos, she insanely submerged there many, many… many torrent years ago.

I listen to the river,
Because it's an elder to me, like my grandfather was, like my grandmother was, like my father was
Like my mother is.

I listen to the river,
Because it whispers journeyed secrets to me, it ripples its origin and destination to my relative, cosmic mind,
It white waters
Its tumbling persistent power
Through every tributary blood vessel of my incarnated soul.
It tells me, that everything that exits its Boca Chica, is a new beginning… like Spring flowering new life…
Like the Arco Iris and its colors, symbolizing hope.

I listen to the river,
Because it beckons me, it washes me, it cleanses me, and it tells me of a John, living there, waiting for me.
He, too, is brave…
Like the river and me.

Child

I, a child… was born on the banks of the Rio Grande.
My mother labored in extreme pain, without even a slightest whimper,
As she pushed with all her will and might, accompanied by the laws of nature
And vilified by the laws of man.
An angel's protective plumed wings kept us hidden from passing patrols.
Swooped the purple sparkling sky,
Flattering from star to star with hummingbird precision
Spraying the heavens with brilliant spectral rain
Keeping a watchful eye, on the anticipating new birth.
Excitingly swooshing, rallying, hovering
With intervals of coaching encouragement outside my mother's womb.
And she, my mother, gritting, grasped the earthen clay where once my father too once lay flat motionless like the chameleon, hidden,
Afraid and concealed against the peering eyes of the law, before continuing his immigrant journey north
Battling desert sand fleas, brush ticks, side stepping side-winding rattlers with poisoned dripping fangs,
Diving headfirst into rat dens looking them straight in the eye as they sniffed their noses at him
He puts a finger to his lips, he says
Quiet…
I'm just as scared as you.

With one final thrust!
Exposing once again, her light within, the purpose of life,
as first defined on the seventh day.
A child… and a child… and a child after child…
consequently, he looked upon me and smiled…
He said I was good. And that I should go out unto the
world and be fruitful!
So, I came to life here as a child!

How I Long for Thee America

How I long for thee America.
As
I willingly traversed unsympathetic and indifferent violent seas to kiss your freedom *Terra*.
As
I chartered across unforgiving blazing desert perils to sip from your sparkling creeks and brooks.
As
I swim the tumbling swollen river with my family clinging to my back like the baby opossums.

How I long for thee America.
As
I faintly hang on to life inside the smoldering belly of the rusty old tubs that can barely stay afloat.
As
I gasp for a bit, any sip, of body heated stench air that keeps me alive inside the suffocating tractor-trailer.
As
I tremble with fear, while I practice over and over the only two words in English I know in the back seat.

How I long for thee America.
As
I tell myself; I do all this to earn a dollar, cutting the grass of a white mansion rose lawn garden.
As
I tell myself; I do all this to earn a dollar, harvesting the farmers' crop under the choking pesticide rain.
As

I tell myself, I do all this to earn a dollar, carrying bricks at construction sites on my back like the burden burro.

How I long for thee America
As
I buzz, to and fro, like the little worker bee, cleaning hotel rooms, toting dirty laundry to the hot steam room for washing.
As
I rush, like the little worker ant, busing leftover smeared dishes in fancy restaurants, back to the hot kitchen for washing.
As
I hurry, like the busy beaver, sweeping chicken poop, cleaning and washing the foul-smelling cages for the laying hens.

How I long for thee America
As
I avoid making eye contact, with any fair skinned person male or female, child or grown-up that may notice my *mestizo* skin.
As
I avoid making conversation, with any fair skinned person male or female, child or grown-up that may notice my *no spic engleesh*.
As
I avoid crossing paths, with any fair skinned person male or female, child or grown-up that may notice my
Nopal immigrant presence.

How I long for thee America
As
I tolerate, all the "dirty-Mexican," wetback, name-calling.

As
I withstand, all the "dumb-Mexican" wetback, name-calling.
As
I endure all the delusional-paranoid-racial-illegal-alien, name-calling.

How I long for thee America.
As
I implore my children to study hard in school, so that they may grow-up to be somebody.
As
I ask my children to observantly study my worn, broken-down body, so that they may strive for a prettier body than mine.
As
I teach my children to study from where we came, where we are, and where we are going.

How I long for thee America.
As
I can see and aspire, to know what standing and walking as a free man feels like.
As
I can see and aspire, for my children what standing and growing up as a free man feels like.
As
I can see and aspire, aspire, aspire, what standing and living as a free man feels like.

How I long for thee America.
As
I see my babies happy and comfortable, because they have food, drink and nourishment in their bellies.

As
I see my babies happy and comfortable, because they blow out the candle to their first-year *piñata* party.
As
I see my babies happy and comfortable, because they learn the pledge of allegiance on their first day at school.

How I long for thee America.
Because
Although you treat me as a nobody, my children shall grow, to become somebody.
Because
Although you treat me as a scum-body, my children shall grow, to become a worthy body.
Because
Although you treat me as an unwanted body, my children shall grow, to become a presidential body.

How I long for thee America!

I'm Back

I swam across the Rio Grande at Matamoros/Brownsville,
Playa Bagdad, Texas.
La migra, was everywhere, they looked right at me but they couldn`t see me.
Man, I'm good!
Weeks later, they do see me, in Houston, and sent me back to my Mexico.
Directly across McAllen/Reynosa, border of Tamaulipas/Texas.
They set me free, to walk across, right there, at the Puente Internacional.
La migra said to me, you are here illegally, so, back to Mexico you go.
Hasta luego mojado.
And I said back.
Hasta la vista baby.

The very same day.
I took the Transporte del Norte bus to Nuevo Laredo.
And the next day after that,
I was washing dishes at Mi Tierra café,
In San Antonio, Texas.
And the week after that,
I was working the boiling hot tar melting machine for a roofing company
In Dallas, Texas.
And the week after, I left Dallas.
I made it to Arkansas, worked for Tyson, plucking and gutting their fattest chickens.
When I finished with the *pollos de* Tyson,

The following week I found myself going southeast for the winter, I picked oranges under the steaming sunshine of Immokalee Florida.

One week before Christmas eve, when all the Florida, oranges were harvested and packed.
Early in the morning, after my first cup of coffee. I visited Kissimmee,
Looking for the first Mexican breakfast taco restaurant I could find.

Parked out front in the small parking lot of Las Cazuelas, I found several *migra* border patrol cars assigned to the area.
I fix my brand-new cowboy, *sombrero Norteño*, tilting it slightly over the right side of my brow, adjust the collar to my also new pin stripe western shirt and walk in wearing my also new leather smell Ostrich boots, with matching belt, holding up my first-time washed Wrangler pant.
I sit at a table close to the front door and order coffee, *Huevos rancheros*, meshed beans and a Flour tortilla.
Mexican American restaurant cooks make the best tasting Flour tortillas. The pretty natural tanned waitress taking my order is a young teenage U.S. born Mexican American *señorita* helping the family-owned business during her time off from school during Christmas vacation.

After wiping the plate clean with the last piece of tortilla. I purposely make eye contact with the *migra* agents chomping down on hot *salsa roja* dripping ham and egg tacos. I grin, show my teeth, push away the plate and coffee cup and run out the door.

After two city blocks of pretend frighten sprint with one arm waving franticly in the wind, a hand holding on down my western tan Stetson *sombrero,* keeping it on my head.
I stop, adhering to the shouts of every *migra* man yelling *alto, alto, manos arriba, manos arriba,* chasing after me out of that taco place.

Three days later, after a long courtesy bus ride on board the *la migras'* green-grayhound, I'm back on the border. This time it's El Paso/Juarez. No matter. I buy a fare and ride a Transporte del Norte bus, to my *ranchito* valley, in the interior, elevated and guarded within the lush crispy cold December Sierra Madre.

At the crossroads drop off. I get off as a proud *Gallo de Palenque Norteño.*
Wearing my ten-gallon felt Stetson, creamy Ostrich boots with matching belt, Rodeo style Wrangler jeans with a plaid snap button long sleeve wrangler shirt, topped off with four pocket black leather vest.

I got dollars in my wallet,
I got dollars waiting in my *casa* with mama,
And I am back where I belong during the Christmas season in Mexico.

And I will return.

Rags

There, upon the Rio Grande's bank,
Are found,
Hastily shed *mojado* swimsuits,
Cast off,
Dumped off,
To accumulate among
The countless other
Multicolored bundles of migrant threads.

There, upon hallowed, sovereign ground
Of the promise land.
Is piled high, wet discarded fabric,
Blending with every
Color of the rainbow,
Brought to this shore
By Mexico's brown spectrum.

The ones who once danced
To the Sun, the Moon, the Wind
And the Rain Gods.

The one's without papers,
The ones who once sang and chanted,
While adored in fine majestic plumes
And royal dyed, golden-laced cloth.
The one's with Tec features.
The one's with the Nopal that Aztlan stamped
Upon their forehead.

The ones who left their river water-soaked clothes
By the Rio's levee,
A kaleidoscope of hopes, wants and dreams
Turned to Rags.

Fence

Halt! Who goes there!
That crawls stealthy towards me.
It is I… *Soy yo*… Jesus.
I am wet, hungry and cold.
I seek to pass, fence… let me pass.
I want to pass,
Para el otro lado.

I have no pass for thee.
Can't you read the sign?
"No Mexicans Allowed."

Limba

Look at them,
How they flock together
Jibber jabbering
All that Zapotec mojo stuff.
See how they stand,
Against the commons locker area wall.
Slapping each other with Jaguar, mixtec, handshakes
With *que onda whey* greetings,
Sent here to study, learn and prosper
By their ancestral King, Montezuma.

They're told back in Mexico,
By the Great Spirit of the golden Eagle.
Before coming here
As reinforcements and replacements,
To precedent Mexican wets,
That they belong here.
That this was once their land
As far as their Sacred Eagle flies.

Feel me, feel my milk of magnesia
KKK rush limba skin.
Feel how their Aztec nopal's spine
Pricks my whiteness
Causing my dark inside
To gush greed and disdain.

O' how I wish ... I could deflower
From all those *nopalitos*,
The yellow, white, pink-orange, red
Blooming cactus flowers
Off their smiling clay-like faces.

O' how I wish … I could take
Those silky-smooth showy pedals
And just throw them
To the ground,
Down there low,
Below my feet,
Where they belong.

And look!
Look how they all walk around
Strutting, like young cock *gallos*
De pelea
Acting like they own the yard.

And they cover themselves
With shirts that have
That Mexican Eagle and snake.
An Aztec warrior and his maiden, embracing…
With all kinds of feathers on their heads.
And Jaguar skins on their bodies,
I guess they think, or believe
The Raptor and Feline
Share some kind of Spirit with them.

And too!
They also wear
The Virgin Guadalupe a lot!
They have her everywhere; on their skin,
Their clothes,
On holy medallions, next to their hearts,
Their cars' dash boards, car windows, bumper stickers,
In their homes…
Religious candles of her, sprinkled with holy water, lit and flickering hope and salvation
Pictures of her hanging on their walls.
In every single church, they worship at
They pray to her,
They even have a special
Day of festive worship, especially for her.

And if you're one of them, and happen to be born
On that her day,
You're named like her
And everybody will call you,
Lupe, or Lupito, or Lupita, Pito or Pita.

It's hard for me.
It's very unacceptably hard for me to understand
Why? Why?
Can't they try … to be
Just like regular "normal" Americans.
If they insist on living like Mexicans,
They should go…. to live in Mexico!
What can I do?!
What can I do?!
What can I do?!

Jose

Jose can you see?
Jose can you see?
Can't you see?
It's not me.

It's not me
That doesn't
Want you
To be free.

Can't you see
It's the law
Of the land
It's outa my hand.

Please try to understand
I'm just one man
You know I'll help you
Whenever I can.

Jose, can you understand?
That you are a Mexican
I am an American
This land is my land
It used to be your land.

As far as I can see,
It now belongs to me
It's no longer free
Not for you, as far as I can see.

Too many Mexicans, here already
Too many Mexicans, here to study
Too many Mexicans, making money
Too many Mexicans, here already

El Ulysses

I cross the scourging sands of Aztlan,
Zigzagging my way through
Cactus fields of dreams.
Dreams of a better life
In the new world of *El Norte*.

El Norte, where opportunities
And dollars, like numbers
Are infinite.

I dodge and hide in the flaming rays
And steaming vapor horizons
From the constant prowling, of
La Migra,

That forces me to camouflage
Myself
Like a false presence upon the land.
Each step that advances me towards prosperity
May be my last.

As I travel through an eco-system
Naturally preserved,
For hardy Desert dwellers… not humans
And since, I, too,
Am considered not human
With my alien label, pre-disposed as
Illegal, thus dangerous… and
Can I be any more-less human than that?

Reduced to creature only status,
I become a brother… to the scorpion,
Chameleon,
Lizard,
Rattler,
Hawk
And all other desert residents
If only for a while.

Until these new
Adopted siblings of my forbidden land
Whisper guidance, directions
And other survival urgings
Out of *la migra's* harm's way.

With clipper feet, the voyage continues,
Towards my desired plotted destination,
El Norte's, urban jungle.
Where milk and honey abounds… and glittered dreams
Are plastered on every concrete façade.

Darting to and fro,
Saving every piece of
Copper, nickel, silver-note, I can.
I do it as an invisible blend
Of that jungle's cemented foliage.
There, existing
As a non-existent inhabitant,
A toiling instrument
That keeps the ivory towers from crumbling.
A minute ant like worker,
Scurrying constantly
Without identity
Until, until,
I
Return once again to my *patria*.
Where at least there,
In my own little Rancho of the world.
I am greeted as a hero, an adventurer!
Like Homer, after his Odyssey.
Me,
A wetback!
Returns to Mexico,
With the greatness
Of
Ulysses!

Picker

Please, Mr. Uncle Sam, man,
Bring back my little wet.
The one you named *bracero*.
I've never known a harder working cat.

Be cool my man Sam,
Don't let my tractors sit and rust.
Bring back the little dude,
Save my ass, don't let it bust.

Come on Unc, my vato,
Talk to that A-say Fox,
Cut a deal with him,
Put some coin, in his secret bank box.

Please, bring my wets back to me!
Damn, how I miss the little spic.
They have the fastest working hands,
Especially, after a swift kick in the ass.

Make it groovy for me Sammy,
Bring back that labor scam
Of turning lettuce into clamies,
Peon stoop labor, I don't give a damn.

Your gray goatee is outa sight!
That hat you style makes it right!
You and me bro, we gotta stay tight!

Sam my man, bring back
My little greaser.
Hoe-say can't you see,
I need the beaner, taco bender.

It's no jive eagle breath!
Depose to me the migrant farm worker,
Can't you see me freaking out!
I need the chili-eating picker.

Mojado

Here I am in New York City, cooking hard and feeling pretty.
With my Guadalupe star, watching over me from afar,
Saving money in a jar, someday I'm going to buy a car.
To drive me to my *Tepeyec*; for us cactus people… that's where it's at.

They want me gone, but here I'll stay, no matter what the legals say.
I'll stay… I'll pay my taxes… and I'll stay.
I'll hide and ride the subway car and jingle money in my jar.
I'll clean the rooms and make the beds and cook tortillas for the feds.

I live and play in Old Chicago, send money home via Wells Fargo,
Selling beer and Wrigley baseball dogs, cleaning dirty restroom stalls,
Cutting ritzy peoples grass, then Sunday mornings go to mass,
Where there, at least, I have some class, although the Bishop, does think I'm less.

I pick your pesticide-soaked melon fields, hired by labor contractors, making deals.
If I don't pick it, who will pick it, will you have your children pick it?
With their pedicure toenails, and their Barbie pony tails,
Riding in their shinny cars, snorting snow like Hollywood stars.

How's your chicken? How's your turkey? How's *la migra*, Mr. Lurky?
I am Pilgrim, I am Tyson, I am the new face on "America's" horizon.

I am here and here I'll stay, no matter what the forked tongues say.
How's your steak? How's your cake? I'll pile your leaves with a Wal-Mart rake.

What happened to the family farm? Guess who paints the old red barn?
What happened to the family tractor? It's driven now by that Mexican Hector.
Who milks Elsie, the jersey cow? Who shears the ba ba little sheep? It's me, it's me
The little wetback, you pay so cheap.
"To market, to market, to buy a fat pig", hurry Juan, hurry Juan, dig-giddy, dig.

Part Aztec, You Say?

Why do Chicanos say?
I'm part Aztec, I'm part Mayan,
We are nothing to them
And they
Tecos, and Mayans are nothing to us Chicanos.

For
If Chicanos and Tecos were of one
Then no Chicano would dare leave
The Tecos, begging
On the streets and International bridges
Of Matamoros,
While
Us Chicanos return to Tejas,
Bellies bloated with
Tecate, Corona beer and *cabrito*,
Feeling righteous and superior
Because we give the
Poor India with
Her dark brown wrinkled and scared begging hand, Two
Quarters,
Two quarters to feed her children,
One baby tied to her back,
A toddler clinging to her falda with one hand
While the other hand, scratches head lice
And yet another of her Teco children
Begging
Two cars ahead of her.

O' yes, sure we brag
Of our Mayan and Aztec heritage
To the white folk on our U.S. side,
And we even
Go
As far as saying
We have Indian blood in us,

When there is Nothing!
Indian about us,

The only Tec, Mayan of us
Is what we read in books
About Aztec history
The films and videos shown to us
By
White, Hispanic and other, history teachers, in middle and high school
Don't say you're something when you're not!
Don't proclaim to be
A child of the *Quinto Sol*,
When you drive and ride in your
Chevy, Ford
Air-conditioned car
Pass the *Quinto Sol*
Burnt little Tec child who begs!

Don't say you have roots in Mexico
When you don't even like Mexicans
And you don't.
Else,
Why do you call them
Wetbacks,
Mojos,
Piojos,
Mojados,
Why do you JOIN?
La Migra, Border Patrol
And beat them back to Mexico
Because it PAYS GOOD?
Does it make you FEEL GOOD?
Else,
Why do you report them to
La Migra?
When you see them domesticating in your neighborhood

No
Chicanito, mio

There is nothing Aztec about us
How can it be?
With a name like
Rudy,
Danny,
Johnny,
Billy
What's so Mayan about those names?

Every day, every night, Tecos and Mayans
DROWN!
In the Rio Grande
While
Migrating to us,
Their descendants for a helping hand,
A job,
A chance for a better life
Like yours, like mine
And what?
What do we do?
NOTHING!
That's what,
Maybe we say
Pobrecito mojadito.
Every day, every night
Our ancestors
FRY TO DEATH!
In the desert
Of the southwest, USA, Aztlan,
COOKED TO DEATH!
By our beloved and famous
Quinto Sol,
And what?
What do we do?
NOTHING!
Just watch the news
And apathetically say
Pobre gente,
Si,
They are *gente*

But remember!
We
Academic, educated, elected to public office
Well-employed, business owner,
Chicanito,
That really and truly
They mean nothing
To you, to us
Those Aztec, Mayans;
So
Don't BRAG!
About the Mayan, Aztec in you
For they walk all around us
And we,
We
Look the other WHEY!

Dos Hermanos

Juan y Juan, Diego y Pablo,
Dos misioneros, dos compañeros.
Uno se viste de manta y huaraches,
El otro de lino y calzados.

El Santo no escribe ni lee.
El Cura, de todo te sabe.
El indio, dedicado a su cerro.
El blanco al mundo completo.

Dos épocas unidas por la Historia.
De dos Juanes especiales,
JuanDiego y JuanPablo II
Escogidos Celestiales.

Uno con Piel de barro, el otro con piel de porcelana,
Ambos con Espíritu Juvenil.
Conectados por medio de brazos Guadalupanos,
Tecos y Contempéranos los dos.

Un santo indígena y el Santo Papa.
Hermanos unidos en Fe.
Refugiados por la Virgen Guadalupana,
Y su verde capa.

Old Mexican

I saw an old Mexican, standing on a bluff, singing back to Mexico,
Cielito Lindo!
He had Jaguar tears, tracking down his bronze leathered cheeks, and he had a throbbing lump in his throat.

I saw the same old Mexican, standing by the riverbank, singing back to Mexico,
Jalisco no te rajes!
He had his arms spread eagle, his face was tilted skyward, and his throat was swollen like the howling Lobo.

I saw a mystic, old Teco Mexican standing high atop the purple shaded, Sierra Blanca, singing back to Mexico,
Mexico lindo y querido!
His entire body was coated in silky emerald green and ruby red hummingbird plumes, brilliant in the western sun.

I saw a young child, of five, maybe six, chasing late spring, early summer dragonflies in his grandmother's Healing-erbal Garden; he sang,
Cielito Lindo!
He was wearing an old worn *sombrero* that once belonged to his grandfather, an old ancient Mexican.

I saw the same boy, of seven perhaps eight, chasing white, red crested roosters in his grandmother's chicken coop. He sang,
Jalisco no te rajes!
He was wearing an old *sombrero*, an asymmetrical necktie, flapping in the wind over his left shoulder as he ran about after the agitated crowned roosters.

I saw a lean lad of nine, close to ten, scampering after
horned frog chameleons, zigzagging in and out of his
grand-mother's blaze blooming, oleander trees.
He sang,
Mexico *lindo y querido*!
He was wearing an old torn *sombrero*, a black necktie
flapping in the wind and a pair of old *vaquero* boots that
once belonged to his grandfather, an old rustic, *Vaquero*.

I saw a youthful man of twenty, twenty-five, standing
straight and tall on a hilltop bluff, looking back to Mexico.
He was singing, "So close, yet so far!"
He wore, a fine, tan, felt, ten-gallon Stetson, a thin
symmetrical black tie clipped to his starched stiff shirt,
Spit polished, black, brand-new bull hide cowboy boots
Over his heart, flashed a shiny U.S. Border Patrol Badge.

El Vendido

There he stood,
All proud and honored and bought
Barato, yet *orgulloso*, to be the center of attention for
someone else`s intention.

In a room filled with us, people
He speaks star-crossed
Selected and chosen and fronted,

By the white rancher, just as it happens, every two years,
for years, and years and years.

His job is to deliver us… to hear some broken, spoken,
Spanish, lies
Glorifying him to mythological status to a room full of
dumbfounded Mexicans,
Gloatingly, proud, to be the one
To tell us why we should vote white and not Mexican.

To remind us, and blatantly, matter-of-factly, point out
The obvious difference in intellectual superiority and of
our inferior oratory limits.
To preach to us… not to think!
Not even for a minute!

That,
Even though we have lived here for generations, after
generations, upon generations,
And that we have forever outnumbered
The "meester" and his sons.
That still, our overwhelming majority's welfare, does not
matter.

Our vote
Should continue to be devoted and deposited for his
master and his masters' sons,
Just as it has always been in the past,
Just as it should be now,
Just as it should always be in the future.

All this
His pre-programmed, rewound, whittled short and small
and dull
Good little Mexican body told us,
Because his rancher owner
Keeps cutting
Him down to small pocket size.

So that he has to meekly peer up.
To his *patron*, with his submissive and accepting "frito
bandito" grin
Readily available for his *jefe's*, occasional good boy pat on
the head

Causing the *vendido*
To forever faithfully, experience, such intense gratification
That he uncontrollably squirts
Piss…
Sprinkling the inside of his pant with yellow wet obedience
Showing us all
That
All he really is, is a *sin verguensa*
Guerkito mion!

And, so…
There he stood, all wet in his pants,
As he spoke in almost very good English
Eulogizing
His beloved rancher.

Convincingly, dramatically, pleadingly
Imploring upon us
That the best man to govern us.
Once again
As it has always been
Is the white rancher.

And, that…
Now, is no real reason to change our poll tax voting ways
Just because
There is at last! And way overdue
A Mexican
Running for election.

After all, when it comes to telling us what to do… who knows best?
And remember!
Who is the one who gives us the jobs!

Pennies a day!
So that at least we can buy rice and beans and maize for tortillas.
So that we can minimally nourish our mal educated bodies.

He!
My *amo*! That's who!
He knows… what our mind's borders should be
Like his father knew,
Like his grandfather knew before him.
The right choice for us is historical!
It's blindly and unquestionably and unconditionally following our rancher
Friend.

It's not, that… Enrique Martinez!

My people!
Mi gente!
I deliver you to him!
I bring you to my *amigo,*
Yours and mine
Thinker.

See him,
See how grand he is,
How strong he is.

As he effortlessly supports me on his lap
With his hand all the way up my ass and to my lips,
I'm his puppet, and he, my puppeteer!
How great!
How good it makes me feel!
He has all my respect, all my admiration, and all my good
little boy devotion.

Come,
Come, all you seemingly citizens,
Follow me,
Follow me to follow him.

I repeat to you!
Do not vote!
For
Enrique…

The one who only sells tacos for a living
How can you begin to compare
A taco bender, beaner, Mexican food seller
To a big establishment rancher.

See my sold-out logic!
Weigh the value of the two
Here… manhandling me, we have the great one, who pulls
my strings

And there… there… you have… ese…ese… Enrique
Martinez, who has no strings…

Let's go with my choice people,
The one
Whom I hope for, and pray for, and beg to, if I have to.

To permit me to visit the inside of his big two-story ranch
house.
That lofty symbol of superiority
I have always desired.

The big white no Mexicans allowed…but yes… dogs are
allowed house.
The house I have always unattainably wondered about
from the distant road
The house I can't get into without you.

Because the big, iron gate is locked to me
And a sign that tells
No Tres Pasen
Trespassers will be shot on sight!

I want too much!
To be asked in
To be invited to sit…!

At their big fancy dining room table,
To eat what they eat
Like I see the big valley Barkleys eat on TV.

With servants and peons, stooped shoulders, inclined
downward heads
Making no eye contact
Sheepishly,
Placing before them, soup bowls and salad bowls and gold
trimmed china plates

Spilling over with many kinds of vegetables, potatoes and other exotic foods.
But no rice and beans!
Maybe some Tostitos chips, to dip in the avocado wacamole, without *frijole*!

And I want to drink from their crystal wine glass, red wine and white and blush wine, the rich man's kool-aide
And after supper.
I want
To go into their smoking room and smoke a big, imported cigar
Hand rolled by Cubans.

I want,
To cock my head back, after a deep savory inhale… and puff out
Silver smoke rings
And see them float up, up, up to the high vaulted ceiling…
But never reaching it because it's too far up there

Por favor my people, indulge me,
I've done everything, to gain their exclusive to me, favor
Everything they have told me to do
I have done it!
I need you!

I need you to do for me,
So that I may continue to do for him!

I have,
Even switched political party
I am now their token Mexican Republican
But only I for now
Not you, not yet
They only take in a few good ones of us, a little at a time.

You stay dumbocrats
Because if you switch party too
My *patrones*, who have me by the *cojones*
Will go off and start a whole new political party exclusively
all their own,
Heavens forbid!

Remember, when they used to all be Brisco Democrats?
Then, we started buying the poll tax and becoming voting
Democrats
Just like them,
Well, not exactly like them… kind of like them…

And we decided, we should vote for Jose Angel
And we did… and Jose Angel was elected
Remember what happened?
They gave up being Democrats,
They turned Republicans.
They said it was better to be a Republican
Rather than vote for Jose the Democrat.

They will certainly be mad at me then
Because I didn't do my job right
I
Didn't make you follow me, to follow them.

They'll spank me,
Punish me,
They'll leave me down here with you
And I'll never get invited to the big house.

Tell me, *mi gente*, what is worse?
To have at least one of us?
Tio Tome
At their disposal to do with you as they please!
Or
Have a *comun y corriente* greaser, political wanna-be
Break the chain
Of *patronismo y chingismo*.

No Señor!
Let us not be the ones to tear the link to servitude!
Do not look for a bright and promising future,

Do not yearn for voting Emancipation!

Let us keep my big white rancher
In his high place…
So that he may continue to keep us
Boot on throat,
Below him…. Place.

Not Good Enough

I'm still not good enough!
My *pocho* Spanish is very rough.
In fact, it's true, I gave it up!
And broke the heart of my darling Pop.

I do not eat the cactus food,
Where once an Eagle proudly stood,
I left behind the Chicano ideal,
I do not know it, I do not feel.

I'm pure Hispanic, your American way
Mono-lingual English just like you say.
My ears can't hear the Spanish sound
My songs are rock, pop with rap abound.

My grandma, she can't talk to me
She speaks that tongue of which I'm free.
She's old and different, she prays a lot
To the Guadalupe that our kind forgot.

I blocked and blanked out my Mexican
And hate to admit that's where we began
Because Mexico, is so *mojo*, so ghetto,
And my name is Freddy... not Alfredo

I can't go back to my fathers' ways.
He pushed me here, but there he stays.
English, English, speak more English,
Brags to his friends, the family I embellish.

So let me study alongside you
And do the work that you do, too.
Don't look at me and see a Mexican,
I try real hard to be an American.

The only thing Hispanic about me
Is a surname by a king's decree.
That hangs about me superficial
As I gladly mispronounce it quite casual.

I did all this; I'm your conformer,
True blue to you, a true transformer
And still you say "not good enough"
To be your American sure is tough!

Prieto

If you only knew what it feels like?
To be incased within this darkened pigmented skin
To be called
Prieto,
Negro,
To be the one rescued from the thrown away trash bin
And reminded of it, *cada pinche dia de mi negra vida.*

To go through life`s cycle
Living just outside the impenetrable "white is right" circle
As the *más prieto de la familia.*

Since the very first time
I
Poked my *pinche cabeza ennegreciada*
With it`s *pinche pelos negros parados*
Out of Mama`s womb
To partake and live, the wonders of life
As
One of God`s creations,
But instead…
To *todo mundo*, it turns out, I`m the inferior one, the coffee grind,
As they turn their shying face away
Once they see my skin, is darker than the rest.

Since then, even before I let out first *grito*
Of which I have many
Rejoicing,
In joining the rest of you
And telling you with my cry
That I`m so happy, so thrilled, so excited!
To be here with you!

That I later learned
I celebrated my initial birthday on my own
Because
I was born too *Moreno* and not *blanco* enough to be
beautiful.

That my birthday *piñata*,
If I got a birthday *piñata* at all
Would not be filled with candy, coins, and little toys,

That my parents, my grandparents, my aunts and my
uncles
Would mischievously teach my siblings and my cousins
To call me Negro! In belittlement sentiment
Thusly, right there and then, I, instantly, was assigned to
the least most status
Within the clan.

Because to be black, is beautiful!
That certainly is true!
But only if you're born African or African American
Not Mexican!
Like me.

Sadly, my Black Opal, Ebony God blessed skin
Is a disappointment of sorts to my people.
Why?
Why?
Are all the fair skinned children of my race
The most preferred, the most admired, the prettiest, the
most intelligent?
Why?
Am I the constant butt of my brothers and sisters put down
jokes
That I was adopted out of abandonment!

Like there will always be something missing from my person,
That something… that not even talcum powder can palely provide,
Like their more complete and more chosen than me,
Because they don't have to powder puff, white make-up powder on themselves
Or rub off the mid-night from their skin.

Even my girlfriends' family pity her because of me,
Because she is genuine enough to give
A *prieto* like me
Her love.
And when she marries me,
They're afraid, they're scared and certain
Her babies will have a fifty - fifty chance
Of being born preferably white.
Or
Pobrecito! Mijito, Prietito!
Not very good odds to their liking.
I hope and pray to God.
That
The *mujer blanca*, love of my life
Gives me babies born *gueros*,
So, that life may treat them kinder
And that they may grow up
To marry,
Gueros and *gueras*
Not *prietos* like me.

Stimulation

Why do you scratch the different parts of your body?
When I pass near you
You even raise your nose to the air, and sniff
What scent do you sense?
What do you see; when you see me with your darting eyes
Is it curiosity or some other mental process?

Unacceptable

Speaking your own mind without saying what's on my own mind… is unacceptable.
You cannot, you will not, you better not! Make a move without a "Mother may I?"
Walk easy, tippy toe around the eggshells I place before you. I've got my eye on you.

And when you stumble and almost fall, I'll stick my foot out, and trip you more.
And when your face does slam the floor. I'll put your fingers across the threshold and slam that door.
Because you are unacceptable. You are unacceptable, know of course that you are unacceptable.

Be Silent Poet

Do not pass on your feelings and thoughts, you call poetry
To your fellow teachers, students, friends
Keep them to yourself.

Suppress

Your embellished imagery, your spoken art.
I have read the many replies
By respondents who say
They enjoy your verses.

Curtail

The sharing of lyrical expressive gifts from the soul
That may bring a smile, a tender thought
To other free spirits among us.

Refrain

From using rhythm cadences, mystical metaphors, cosmic visions
To nourish the boundless mind numbed by oppressive
Practices aimed at rendering people submissive
Stoic, mechanical, frontal lobotomy type.

Cease

The use of vivid poesy to stir and arouse the pleasure senses
That yearn for the warm feeling of an amorous embrace
Savoring the unbridled sensation of a passionate kiss.

Subdue

The use of romantic verse to stimulate the body being
Losing itself in the dizzied spinning of climatic ecstasy
Sensually collapsing in the loving arms of a Valentino.

Hold

Sending desirable messages about spending memorable
days and eves on a deserted beach
With someone you love, or like, or someone you desire to
meet; casting yourself away
Under tall swaying fruiting coconut trees, periodically
breaking from your love making
To cool off in turquoise water before returning for more

Forget

About suggesting to an indefatigable wife, mother, to
pause briefly during working hours to Think of how she
will rush home, cook, feed the children; help them with
their homework,
Bathe them clean with the thoughtful anticipation before
putting them to bed
So that she may then bed her mate, consummating, their
nuptial vows
Then reposefully sleep next to him, till the predawn
morrow
Waking with a stretching smile, because of yester-night.

Stop…

Be silent poet.

Beat on Ese

To all the ones that said you couldn't do it
This E-JE… is for them.
To all the ones that said you couldn't do it
And anticipated the moment to say, "I told you so"
This E-JE… is for them.
To all the ones that brought nay-nays to your planning meetings.
This E-JE… is for them.
To all the ones that said, if you do it "no one will come."
This E-JE… is for them.

To the ones that said, "You can do it!"
This A-JUA!… is for them.
To the ones that helped you make it so
This A-JUA!… is for them.
To the ones whose cheers helped you across the finish line
When you thought you couldn't reach it
This A-JUA!… is for them.
To you, for setting goals and working hard to reach them
This A-JUA!, this A-JUA! and these A-JUAs!… are for you.

Crossover

Y volver, volver
Voooollllveeeer
To *rancheras, cumbias, baladas, chotis*
Huapangos, redovas, valse
and
Polkas
To
Gritos of Joy,
Pain
Or
Sorrow
Or
Maybe
Just remembering days *de Ayer*.
Con Mariachis reaching
Way deep inside you
And dancing,
And singing
Jalisco no te Rajes!
With your Jaguar-Eagle soul.

Singing
For a better tomorrow
While you
Volver
And swing with Goodman
For a good time...
Jazzing
This wonderful life
With Louie,
Feeling smooth and fine
When moody or blue
With Holiday,
Scatting up town
With Ella,
Then

Taking her dancing
Your way
With old blue eyes.

Rocking
With the king,
Rolling with stones and Beatles…
You Grammy the tunes
Of all the latest bands.
Crossing two lands
And with you
Music,
Yes, Music
The boogie woogie bugle boy
And
His Andrews sisters.
You crossed over,
While on leave
From dodging Hitler's, Mussolini's and Hirohito's
Nazi, Fascist and Imperialist bullets.

Crossing back again with
Pedro Infante, José Alfredo Jiménez, Chelo Silva and Lola Beltrán
Zooting yourself all up
To show them all
A dandy *tiempo*
A-todo-dar.

You are the Bridge,
The Connector,
The Ambassador,
The Foundation,
The Continuation,
To the crossover,
To multi-culture,
To the sweet, blended rhythm…
Of *Amerchicanismo*.

To Your Health

Salud, America!
To your Health!
Another Tequila, *con Sal y Limon*.

Salud, America!
To your Health!
Another Cuba Libre.

Salud, America!
To your Health!
This Bud is for you.

The Good Old Days

Do you remember?
The good old days
Do you remember?
The good old boys
Do you remember?
The old *patron*,
Do you remember him *bien carbon*!

Do you remember reading?
"No Dogs and No Mexicans allowed!"
Do you remember, being told, during corporal punishment…
"No *speaking* Spanish in school allowed."

Do you remember?
The spic.
Do you remember?
The greaser.
Do you remember?
The *dumb, dirty Mexican, the beaner, taco bender.*

Yes,
Those were the good
Old days.
They're gone now, aren't they?
Never to return, will they?
Never forgotten!

3 – Schools & Education

Friend

Daddy, there's a little boy
In school with me
He came in yesterday,
The teacher said
He's from Mexico
And asked us all to say hello.

His name is Montezuma
Like the Aztec King
But we'll call him
Monty…for short
We all like him
He's part of our court.

And daddy, he doesn't speak
Any English at all.
But he's really good
With numbers
And quite popular
With the soccer team players.

He brought his lunch to school
But it wasn't a sandwich,
He called it
A taco, tortilla
We traded, we ate, and it was great!

After school, I said my good-bye
And
I'll see-ya
He said,
Si,
I'll see-ja

I think he's smart
He learns really fast
I'll help him study
For our next spelling test.

That's nice buttercup,
Do welcome him.
Mexico,
Is a long, long way from here.
Be his friend, show him
That here in America
There is nothing
To fear.

Two Teachers

Two teachers talking in the lounge
Sipping coke, and coffee too
Munching chips with poly-grip
Smacking dentures yellow green

Asking questions to themselves
Loud enough for all to hear
Why do we have to teach?
Non-English speaking
Illegal,
Wets,
Why don't they just stay away?
Don't they know, they make us think
Don't they know it's harder work
For us to see them here for free
Eating cafeteria food
Using desks for learning skills,

Don't they know it's hard for us
To see them laughing with their friends
In those foreign cheerful smiles,

Don't they know it's hard for us
To hear their Spanish with our ear
We know they're talking about us
Cause we can read them like a book.

We wish they'd just would go away
But we know they're here to stay
And us "Americans" will have to pay
With our tax dollars and peace of mind.

So, on and on the story goes
In teachers lounges near and far
Teachers asking questions why?
Knowing what the answers are

Hoping still someone would say
We closed our border down Mexico way
With *La Migra* patrolling night and day
Every freaking inch along the way
From Brownsville, Texas, to San Diego/L.A.

Dreaming of that utopic day
When no more *mojos* in their class
No more colors, clay-like brown
Coming in and sitting down
English spoken all the time
You and yawl and yes and yeah
We and us and just because

This is America, and it is ours…
We took it from them fair and square
Killing, stealing, lying, lynching,
Raping, shooting and back-stabbing.

Two teachers talking to themselves
In their private little worlds
Enclosed behind the lounge room door
Protected from the outer gore

Of kids and kids and still more kids
Of wets and wets and still more wets
That come in waves, big tidal waves.

And give them work that makes them think
Of how they hate the little spic
That one day soon will finish school
And graduate from college too

And then invade their teacher's lounge
And have to hear them once again
To laugh with their peers, bilingual smiles
Knowing that it's still real hard

To hear those Spanish spoken words
To wonder if they're meant for them
Those laughing, unknown laughing words
That pierce their English only ears

While sitting with their poly-grip
Of smacking dentures yellow green
Thinking of what might have been
Without the wets and all the mexs.

A perfect world, a perfect job…
Behind the doors to teacher's lounges
Two teachers sit and think aloud.

How Old Is She?

No one really knows how old
She is.
But she sure does look old,
Under those Mexican dresses
She wears to school every day
She looks older
Than the rest of us,
Because her feet,

Her feet, give her age away.
Like thirty maybe? Maybe more…?
You can tell by
Looking at her toes… sticking out from her *huaraches* made
of some kind of animal hide leather,
Or something,

Her toenails are thick, like the first communion bible, my
Padrinos give me when I was eight.
And they are some kind of brownish color, or something…
Like the color of
Old nails you find in your father's toolbox
The bended nails, he never
Wants to throw away, because he says to you
He may have a use for those rusty old nails someday.

She's old
Because
Her hands tell me so
Her fingernails are short and flat, like thumbtacks, and
they don't pass the tip of her fingers
Like mine and my sister's do
And her hands, and her fingers
Are kinda plump
Like the janitor lady that works here
But only her hands
And her fingers are plump

Not she,
She's skinny.

Maybe she's skinny
Because
She doesn't eat very much.

In the cafeteria, during breakfast and lunch
She only takes a few bits off her food tray.
Then, when she thinks nobody is looking
She, very quickly, like a cat, an ocelot, or something…
Paws what's left on her tray into some paper towel napkins
The brown ones
The rough kind of paper towel napkins
The ones our school principal puts for us
In the rest rooms
And she sticks the leftovers in her purse of many colors,
made from straw, or something…
I guess she must have a doggie at home she takes her
leftovers to, or something, or maybe, someone…

I really think she's old
Because
She doesn't show us
Her face,
She doesn't look up much at all,

She mostly looks down
And her hair looks down a lot too
They both do.
Except one time, one morning, I remember…
She looked up, and
I was able to see her whole entire face
It was a pretty, native, face
Like the beautiful cactus blossoms of her homeland
And her hair looked up too
They both looked up when she heard someone say
Hola Rosa, Buenos Días…como estas?

She shyly and somewhat surprised answered back
Meekly,
Bien gracias.

And when *bien gracias* opened her mouth
I think it was on accident or something...
I saw she had some kind of shiny metal... golden yellow, bordering
One of her front teeth,
The kinda shiny metal, olden people
That go to the dentists in Mexico come back with between their teeth.
At first, I thought it was
Gold
What she had between her teeth
And I thought that people who put gold in their mouth like that, must have a lot of money or something...

Until one day
When I asked my social studies teacher,
Mr. MacCain, do people from Mexico that use gold on their teeth
Have a lot of money?

He answered back
No,
There's no more
Gold
In Mexico.

We got it all out of there a long time ago
The only
Gold
Left in Mexico now
Is what those people are able to find
And stick it... between their teeth
But don't worry
Some day when they die,

We'll get that
Gold
Too.

So, every day I wonder
Whenever I see her in school
I wonder… how old is she?
She hardly ever talks
So she tells nobody
And the kids barely ever talk to her
So they don`t ask

She sure looks like she's been around a long, long time, or something…

No Habley

When I first came to school here four years ago
I had a teacher/coach by the name of *No Habley*!
My cousin, Roberto, was his student the year before me.

Roberto, who knew his way around school
"Like he knew the back of his wet back hand,"
Introduced me, he said hey coach, look
This is my cousin Juan, he, *No Habley*, patting my back.

The *No Habley* coach, chawed-out a bunch of smelly
tobacco juice spit words,
To which, I had no idea what they meant.
In fact, not even the people who did *habley*, understood
what he said.
So for my first six academic weeks in school,

I thought I was special because
The coach, was kind enough
To call me by his name every time he saw me
He said, hey, *No Habley*!

My Magic

A brand-new school year, I barely, just started today
And thank God for school uniforms
And thank God for my mother,
She brought to me, two sets,
That she bought for me
At the garage sale.

One I wear today
And the other I'll wear tomorrow,
While she washes the one, I'm wearing today.

She brought to me
A pair of washed and clean and in very good shape
Nikes
That she bought for me
They fit just right.

And she brought to me
What she bought for me
From Wal-Mart,
A brand new
Backpack
Never been used by nobody.
This is yours *Mijo*!
She proudly tells me, as I put it to my nose.

I smell, then inhale, the new backpack smell.
YES! My brand new, very own, backpack
And look, she says, it even has some kind of tag
So that you can put your name on it.

This *mochila* brings with it magic, for one whole entire
school year I hear her say.
And look inside it *Mijo*, and find things…
And whatever you put into it
And whatever you take out of it
Will become your magic, *Mijo*.

My La Mees

My La Mees, E.S.L. (English as a second language) *ingeeish*,
Teacher,
Tells me
That *chee* too, can spic Spanish.
I say to myself, yeah-right, you *weesh*.

It was my first day at school…
Sixteen years old, had barely come over from Mexico
Never in my life, had I felt so scared, so low.

I didn't even have too much school supplies,
Just a pen, a pencil and some *papel*, no papers… and my
hungry, starving, craving mind.
And the La Mees, Thank God! Who turned out, to be color
blind.

I found, that educational inclusion was my Teacher's
mission,
I learned this, the moment she started calling the class roll
And to my surprise! Every "R" she knew to roll.

So, from that day on, I peered her every move, with my
Jaguar-Eagle eyes,
As she moved and glided, all across the salon teaching.

She knew everything! Like Socrates and Plato!
And she had the grace of a Prima Ballerina!

From that day forward, I adopted her as my *Madrina*,
But it was my secret that I kept to myself…
How I fell in love with such a most smart! Beautiful! And
kind Beauty!

Clinging to her total word, that musically floated to my ears, like a Dove's soothing cooing.
A smile, that DaVinci, would divorce his Mona Lisa for!
And when she danced and pranced by me... the sweetest, cleanest, scent...
I never smelled before!

My La Mees,
E.S.L. *ingeesh* Teacher
Always made me feel as a welcome student, a learner,
Inside her classroom, I pretended, I was Romeo, and she, my Juliet.

I belonged to her... to her, I wasn't a foreign alien.
She always made it safe for me.
She never, ever, cared, my back was wet.

On The Back of a Burro

Dear principal, O' my dearest school principal
I come to you, sitting upon a burro's back
His head drags low, so that I may someday… be able to stand straight and tall.
He works his fingers to the bone; his body is a bent and ratchet wreck.

He dresses me in the cleanest school attire
Scorching his bare back underneath the noon day fire.

Protecting my tender feet; he provides the leather-patent shining bright
And he does toil, from pre-dawn morning light, way passed sunset, and into night.

Unto my fur soft delicate hands, a pencil he does place
And under my arm, a slate for my scribing.
An apple for my teacher, and a lunch pail filled with nourishment for me.
And he? Well, he just continues laboring hard; exclusively for me.

Dear principal, O' my dear, dear, Principal.
I come to you, upon a burro's back. He never complains, he simply keeps tugging the tow.

Someday, *mijita*… he says to me; some glorious day in your future; he repeats to me.
One very fine day, during the month of May, He says to me… that, his head shall never again hang low
When during my graduation, alas! He tells me… he shall be seated, in the very front row!

I can see him now…

So proud, and so Strong, so Tan, and so very clean, and so Perfectly Groomed! Just like the Beautiful,
High Stepping, Caballo Ballo, de Antonio Aguilar!

My Friend Martha

Martha doesn't like going home after school
She says she hates her life.
She wishes her family was like my family.
She wishes her *Tio Meme* didn't have to live with them
She says she hates him.

He came to live with them when she was barely five years old.
He was fifteen.
He came to live with them because her mother needed a babysitter.
Her mother works nights at Gencho's dance club.
Before Gencho's she worked at Cuatro Amigos down by the shrimp docks,
Before that she worked at Mario's
She says her mother is a *cantinera*.

Martha says her mother comes home late every night
Always at two or three in the morning,
Never earlier than that.

She stays awake lying in her bed every night until she hears her mother come home.
Her family lives at the Johnny Joe's apartments,
She hates it there, too.

All the apartments are small, cramped and too close to each other, you can hear everybody's everything.
They have too many roaches and lots and lots of rats running around everywhere.
They smell bad too, like the old abandon falling down shrimp house across the street where the homeless winos live. She says the dirty water from the restrooms doesn't go to the pipes that are under the ground when they flush the toilet.

The pipes are broken, and the restroom water makes stinky *charcos*
On the backside of the apartments by the alley.
The owner doesn't want to fix the broken pipes because he says that the people that live in the apartments break the pipes and the restrooms.

She has a little sister, ten years old and a little brother, eight.
Martha is thirteen years old, but she looks more like eighteen, maybe nineteen.
She makes her little sister sleep in the same bed with her because of their *Tio Meme*.
She makes her little brother sleep on the same bed with them too; he sleeps at their feet
She keeps the door to their bedroom closed at night.
The door lock doesn't work so every night when they go to bed
She has to push the *comoda*-dresser against the door to keep her *Tio* from coming in when they are in bed, and he knows her brother and sister are asleep.

My friend Martha doesn't like going home after school
But she has to; she is always the first one to get on the bus.
She sits on the very front seat to the right of the bus driver
As soon as the bus stops at Garriga Elementary where we get off.
She is the first one to get off, walks as fast as she can to get to her apartment where her little sister is waiting for her outside on the steps.

She is very concerned for her little sister and gives her strict orders never to go inside until she gets there.
Because their mother is asleep and her *Tio Meme* is awake, waiting for the little sister to go inside.

My friend hates her *Tio Meme*.

Fernanda

Fernanda, has a growing secret.
She brings it to school every day.
She walks the halls, and when
She's not, she's throwing up in the
Restroom stalls.

Fernanda, still wants to wear her denim, blue jean mini
falda.
But she can't, so she wears big baggy shirts and khaki
pants instead
Because there's something inside of her…
It punches, it stretches, it twists and turns and even
Gives an occasional *patadita* or two.

What's wrong with Fernanda?
She no longer moves like la J-Lo, Lady GaGa, or la
Madonna.
And Fernando, her *novio*, doesn't hip-hop,
Like L.L. Cool J with her anymore either,
Before when the school year had barely just started
You would always see them *abrasando y besando*
everywhere
On campus
They were always a happy, loving couple.

Pero, Fernanda, Fernanda,
En dónde está tu mini *falda*, Fernanda?
There is something different about you Fernanda,
I don't know what?
Your hair and your face, they seem to have a shiny glow
about them
Like la Angelina Jolee!
You really look beautiful, your body does too!
But your look, your *mirada*, your *mirada*, has a puzzled
maze upon your face.

Is it true Fernanda, is it true?
Is what they are saying about your secret true?
Tell me your secret Fernanda, tell me, you can tell me.
I'm your friend; I'm your almost, practically best friend,
Except for that time when I danced with your boyfriend Fernando
At the *Quinciañera* dance, de Rosa Betancourt
And you got mad at me and called me the "B" word.

You know that if I had a secret like yours, I would tell you.
I would surely tell you, Fernanda.

Self Concept

What is it about me GOD
Why must I always feel this odd?
I'm just a normal teenage boy
It's not my fault *en donde estoy.*

My parents brought me here for school
But Chicanos call me a *mojo* fool.
I go to hide way deep inside me
But there a *"pinche* wetback" is all I see.

It seems as if I'm real contagious
Because the way I'm avoided is so outrageous.
The principal really didn't welcome me
She said I'm a drop-out statistic waiting to be.

A minus number towards the school's "exemplary status"
She said my presence here will eventually hurt "us."
It's never my intent to harm anyone…
I simply want to study, be a good son.

But why, do these Chicanos hurt me so?!
They continuously say "back to Mexico, I should go."
If they only knew, how I miss my *Tierra*
Because there, at least, *no soy un qualquiera…*

They laugh at me whenever I speak.
Gawking at me like a carny's side show freak
The way I dress is not in style
I'm always judged, I'm always on trial.

My days at school are really torture
I feel, as if I'm an academic poacher.
Please, help me Dear God, to understand
The ways and customs of this new land,

Return my pride, my self-esteem
And to my principal I shall redeem
My use of her books, desks, and cafeteria food
And prove to her how she misunderstood,

That I'm just another normal boy
And *aqui me quedo, y no me voy*
What's really sad and odd to see
Is that my principal sure looks
A lot like me.

The Heavenly Ones

You are the quiet ones.
The ones teachers love to have in class.
The ones who just sit there without ever talking
Smiling shyly at the cool kids' put-down jokes… and you are the ones who never squeal.
When the burnt-out teacher wants to know who bulls-eyed his chalk dust coated, black rimmed glasses
With a chewed-up spit wad,

You are the noiseless ones.
The ones school principals love to have in school.
The ones who never get sent to the office, therefore, he can't put your name and your face together
Even though he daily stands right next to you in the cafeteria during breakfast and lunch,
Looking past you, to the apples of his eyes… the pretty ones… who talk loud… who act proud…

You are the minimum requirement ones.
The ones who school counselors have the easiest time with.
The ones who are satisfied with whatever class schedule is handed them
And forgotten about, until next semester, when another quick fix for school is given to them
On a blue tone paper, with class subjects, room numbers, and a book locker number one twenty-five,
With a right thirty-one, left to five, right to twenty
Combination… that doesn't work… you know it doesn't work…
Because you have had that same book locker for the past three years, and every year, you return to the same locker, try to open it, but it never opens.

But you're the only one that knows your book locker is jammed shut

So you tote all your books with you from class to class and everybody thinks you're weird
Because you never complain… because you're neither nerdy nor flirty.

You are the not to bother with ones.
The ones whose telephone numbers are never asked for,
The ones who ride the bus to and from school, sitting on the same exact bouncy seat, day in and day out,

The ones bus drivers love and look forward to shuttling every day.
And he smiles with you, as you load and unload his yellow transport…
Because he knows it wasn't you who threw the broken piece pencil to the front of the bus
And hit Mary on the head
Or hid Sid's backpack, way in the back and he had to pull the bus over to the side of the road and find it, for Sid,
Who was crying…

You are the non-yearbook ones.
The ones who never spend their saved-up money on the school annual,
The ones who never get asked to sign someone's face, "good luck" "friends forever"
Love Wanda.
At your high school graduation, when your name is called, and you confidently walk across the commencement
Stage, to proudly receive your diploma.
The principal shakes your hand, smiles at you for the first time in four years and inquiringly thinks to himself
Before the next name is called
O, so this is Celeste… what a pretty face… I never knew… I always wondered…
Who Celeste was…

Celeste… the one with the Heavenly name…

Eagle & Jaguarandi

A teeny, tiny bird,
Was brought to my classroom today.

The principal said
He was from the Eagle family,

That just recently
Migrated here from Mexico.

The coolest, sleekest, prettiest
Cat
Enrolled in my freshman English class today.

When I spoke to her
To welcome her.
She smiled at me *feliz*.

When I asked her, her name?
She said her name
Is Jaguarandi.

Val

Otra vez la mula al maiz
y
otra vez pinche disgrace.
en estos hallways *del escuelin*
Soy un mojado, Valentin.

Gabachos say, don't let him in
Chicanos say, I don't fit in.
They both avoid me like Anthrax
When I'm around them I can't relax.

They look at me from head to toe
Glaring, saying my class is low.
They pound and pound me with their words
They even use their hands for birds.

In every crevice of my house,
There seems to live a little mouse.
And even he will run away
Looking back, he calls me "Whey!"

So here I am in the land of plenty
Scorned and cursed by sooo many…
Living here because mama and papa,
Brought me over *con el coyote's mapa*.

I don't belong, I don't, I know
Yet I sway and go with the flow,
Learning everything, I am
Like *pollo, piojo, mojo* and damn…

I'm wet, illegal and even an alien.
I'm all those things, not even human.
Teachers, they all yell at me.
They say they're teaching me for free!

They do not know I have a job,
They think I'm here just to rob.
They think I'm stoned when in class, I nod.
But I spend my nights cleaning rooms next to God.

I try to stay among the shadows,
As I admire the migrating swallows,
Free and oblivious of any borders
Unlike me and my Mexican brothers.

Who landed here from another World
And then, these two, have me totally swirled.
An alien from a third world country
With *La Migra*, always giving me the third degree.

I do not like the forked tongue
That uses me as a climbing rung.
This is "America" so speak "American"
When I'm around them I can't speak Mexican.

I dread that morning bell for class
And hate myself for feeling less.
I wonder as we salute the flag,
Shall I have esteem someday, to brag?

That once I walked these *pinche* halls,
And made it out because I have balls!
To them proclaim, to hell with shame,
To proudly say Valentine is my name!

I want to be like many others,
An uprooted Mexican, replanted here by their fathers.
To grow and prosper and then give fruit
And too my children, for them to root.

To cultivate them with this soil
And help all those who come here to toil.
To ease their pain of feeling odd
To pray to Mary and the almighty God.

But now I'm stuck in this *escuelin*
Becoming Val, and not, Valentine,
Always sleepy, always tired,
Always hoping I won't get fired.

We save our money to buy a house
And keep a cat to catch the mouse.
I, shall survive, I shall endure,
I'll make it out rest assure.

Immigrant Student Prayer

Virgencita Santa,
Let me go to sleep in peace tonight.
And during my reposeful slumber
Send to me, *Angelitos,*
But, let them be *Angelitos Estudiosos*!
Tutors of the English language.

Let these angels of scholarship,
And even let the Saints of Universities
Come to me while I rest
From my daily toil at school.

Let them instruct into my snoozing mind
Not how to fruitlessly tally sheep
But the solving of Arabic numbers in English instead.

Let them practice and repeat to me
The sounds of a-e-i-o-u and consonants
While we sail into intellectual infinity
Whispering back and forth,
Nouns, pronouns, verbs, adjectives and adverbs.

Let my sleep be not spent in vain nighttime reverie
Tangled in confusion between my beloved Castilian
And my now acquiring English.

Instead allow my Spanish lips
Kiss and Romance the English Queen`s idiom
And may we dance and prance round the Maypole
In colorful rhythm and harmony.

One Teacher

She shyly entered my classroom, with an official piece of paper in her left hand,
Stepping gingerly towards me trying not to make a sound, as she kept her culturally nervous eyes away from me, preferring instead to seek some solace by looking down.
I too looked there as she did, but unlike her; I knew we both shared the same and equal common ground. Two pairs of feet were what I found, mine were grown and my shoes more worn,
Hers youthful, petite, brand new shinny patent leather barely making a sound.

Her bashful, young, sun cast arm, extended towards me the authorized note from the Principal's office with Instructions scribed on it. Though I could not fully see her juvenile tender face, I thought, maybe it was a youthful passing faze.
Her slender fingers trembled so, like when the frightened newborn first shows its instinctual crying face. She reflexively pulls her bronzed hand back, returning it clinched to her side, eyes down cast, still, looking to the ground.

I say to her, welcome, and please, young miss, do take a seat, they call me Mr. "T"
And please, young lass, do tell us all, for we are curious, truly wishing to know, we need to know,
How may we call thee?
She meekly replies, slightly raising her clear hazel eyes, please dear sir, thou and they, may call me Marie.
She finds a desk unoccupied, next to the eastern window and outside next to the window, a tall, shady, ancient oak. She sits, keeping her vision, private thoughts away from the teacher and rest of the class, instead, focusing on the mighty oak tree.

The days pass, seasons come, seasons go, and so too the years and young Marie, kept coming back, always choosing to sit on the eastern side of the room, until one sunny day during the fainting days of May, she realized that her time had arrived to part from her very familiar and comfortable surroundings and too from her friend the old oak tree.
She stood from her desk straight and sure, commencing her walk towards the next journey in her life, better prepared to meet the next challenge of other unknown fears.

She exited proudly, carrying with her a bond piece of paper printed in bold, stamped with an official golden seal, regally bound in fine smelling leather.
She kept her eyes straight; she no longer looked down, for she has toiled and sowed for her a bright new path...
I too, looked straight ahead just as she did, for another young life and I, were now forever entwined. And so, I too a new path have found.
I heard and I listened to her firm parting steps, click-tapping, click-tapping, heel-toe, heel-toe
I listened, I heard as it faded away, the sound of a young girl's click-tapping, heel-toe, heel-toe
As she proudly walked away.
I went to the window and looked out at the tree; I said to us both, "What a beautiful sound!"

The Dropouts

How long has it been?
How many have we let go?
Who fell between the cracks?

Can we count them all?
In one hand,
Or hands, or toes?

Where did they come
From?
Where did they go?

Do we really want
To know?
Please… don't tell me so

How much longer will it be?
How many more
Before we see,

That out of every
Hundred
We drop fifty.

School Prayer

Bless us dear Lord, for all the little Eagles,
For they swoosh into our lives on the first day
Of school, to make us happier and richer.

Bless us dear God, for all the tiny Jaguars,
For they pounce forth juvenile enthusiasm
In our classrooms to make them merrier.

Bless us dear Jesus, for all the young Lions,
For they step as adventurous esquires through our halls of academia
Reminding us of dignity and pride, at its' commencement.

Bless us O' Holy Ghost, for all the melodic Golondrinas,
For they sing purely from the heart, flying swiftly and unbound
As they remind us of the journeys yet to come.

Bless us Sacred Trinity, for all the wise Owls
For they patiently teach and re-teach, advise
And encourage; that wisdom is there for the taking.

4 – Hope ♥ Faith ♥ Love

Soledad

Fuiste muy mala conmigo, traicionera Soledad.
Cuando solo, triste y abandonado me dejaste,
Allí, por la Oria dese nublado y tempestuoso mar
Y tú, tranquila huiste,
Siguiendo ese otro supuesto amante.
Cual tus malvados ojos negros
De esmeralda verde te pintaba,
Con lujuriosas intenciones disfrazadas
Con la astucia de su dulce palabras.

El viento frio e indiferente de esa costa mar,
La espuma salada y ligera remolinaba
Al redor de mi triste y existente penar.
Mientras, tú figura cautivadora y hechicera
Se alejaba más lejos de mí con cada uno
De tus pasos coqueta.

Quise correr para impedir
Tu separación ansiosa de mí, así a él.
Pero algo en mí dentro y profundo sentido
Detuvo mis pies clavados en la arena.
Quede, estoico, viendo tú rompiendo partir.

Al fin; de mi vista desapareciste
Y muy lejos de mi te apartaste
Llevando contigo mi amor.
Derramándolo sobre tus burlonas huellas
De esa playa que en un tiempo
Fue nuestro sitio favorito de tantos
Besos, carisias y encanto.

Viene la siguiente ola corriente estrellándose
Enzima de aquellas, tus últimas imprentas desviadas
Borrando para siempre nuestro acoplamiento.

Te fuiste con ese maldito Soledad.
Dejándome con el corazón cicatrizado
Y mi melancolía Soledad…
Pasa el tiempo Soledad, y conozco
Un Nuevo y dulce amor llamada Consuelo
¡Te amo Chelo!
¡Adiós! Soledad.

El Ultimo Adios

Me fui rompido, roto y atontado,
Tropezando sin rumbo y dirección
Por este golpe que tú me has dado
En el mero centro del corazón.

Mi vista pañosa, casi ciega,
Por las lágrimas que inundaban mis ojos,
Y aunque lo que me paso es historia vieja
Que se ha repetido en muchísima gente sobre todos los tiempos.

Siempre, el último adiós, es el que duele más.

I Wrote Your Name

Walking home from school one day.
I wrote your name on the passing spring breeze.
I used my forefinger, just as the orchestra conductor,
Uses his flowing baton to extract symphonic music
From his players to spell out the lyrical, articulated,
Sonant, alphabetic letters to your name.

Phonetically, I pronounced each syllable with ease.
Ri-ta-Ca-ta-li-na; *la chica más bonita de la escuela.*
Ri-ta-Ca-ta-li-na; *la niña Reyna de mi amor.*
Ri-ta-Ca-ta-li-na; *mi futura novia.*
Ri-ta-Ca-ta-li-na; *te quiero mucho.*

So, soft it did flow, sailing off on the wayward wind,
Your name I mean, your name I say.
Lifting higher and higher, like the Peregrine rocket,
Gliding higher and higher, like the Condor in flight.
Sent by me to travel the skies around the Globe
Hoping someday the musical signature of your name
Returns in your person back to me.

I looked all about me; once assured that I was alone.
I shouted out, the source of such juvenescence feelings,
Pretty Catalina, Pretty, Pretty, Rita Catalina!

It was pleasant to me, the sound of your name.
I had pronounced and spoken it privately, many times
before.

Each time I said it, the spinning spun prettier; never the same,
Over and over and over, I said it again, more and more.

And off it went, like a dancing feather in the wind, waltzing
To and fro, your name I mean, your name I say…

Adios, sweet name, fair Rita Catalina. Till tomorrow morning… in Miss Garza's class.
When she scrolls the class roll, calling out each student there.
I shall await with much anticipation as she finally says "Rita Catalina"

You answer, "*Presente*, Maestra," and once again, my skin goose bumps,
At the sound of your *patron*'s namesake, followed by the soft melody, of your voice.

Summer Gardenia

I shall never ever take in more memorable juvenile scents,
As the evening bloom of your very first gardenia smell,
That you in my direction, once upon a time, have sent
During the fateful summer eve when I for you befell.

Your loose, mother of pearl linen dress, white, like the Luna mar,
Flirtingly flapped in the breeze, whiffing welcomes towards me.
As you freshly strolled the church grounds of a warm summer bazaar.
Being very familiar with gardenia perfume… I, like a buzzed honeybee, in Grandmother's Garden, thirsting for an itty-bitty sip of your sweetness began to respire.

The chaperoning summer wind, stirred your flower's nectar over to me your threshold to womanhood that extolled such balminess,
Unfolding and releasing right before me your full moon bouquet,

Of the summer gardenia.

Mestizo Newly Weds

High atop the pyramid of the sun,
Surrounded by the sprawling metropolis of Tenochtitlan,
Two *Mestizo* newlyweds, stand bathing with the Aztec sun.
They join hands; raise their clay like faces to the pastel Celeste sky…
And pray; Heavenly Father, bless us, "Thy will be done."

Below their sandaled feet, reverberates tribal beating hearts,
Of millions of long-ago ancestors, chanting songs, trading wears,
With jiggling dance steps, keeping time with cadence drums.
Celebrating in co-habitation, the mystical wonders of the universe.

Two young lovers far removed from the glorious past,
Of gilded Omnipotent Emperors, Crowned Plumed Princes and Princesses,
Brave warriors dressed and decorated with spirited Jaguar skins.
Arrows straight, flawlessly feathered for accuracy like the hawk and eagle eyes.

The cool evening arrives, and they move to the pyramid of the Moon summit.
They join in body and soul, pledging their eternal, fertile love.
Embracing; they renew the vows they took before the alter of the holy church,
Of Our Blessed Lady Star of the Sea.
They slowly rotate, romantically embraced in place,
Beneath, the vision and loving grace of God.
Jointly, renewing their marriage vows to their *Mestizo* love.

Brindis

Te brindo mi amor, hoy en este día de las madres,
Con la tinta roja
Que corre por mis venas.
Desde hace muchos, muchos años
Ya pasados y remetidos,
A mi vieja y antigua memoria.
Desde aquellos dulce tiempos
Cuando tú estabas entre niña y mujer,
Yo siempre te quise.

Recuerdo bien y claro y para siempre,
Aquella ves cuando por primera ves
Te espié sentadita en el perfumado, floral jardín de tu casa,
Rodeada por gran multitud de flores, y todos aquellos
bellos colores del arco iris.
Y cienes y cienes de pinto reste mariposas flotando,
parparían do alegre
Como confeti, volando, sobre el aire, valsando a tu
arreador
Embragadas por tomar el dulce néctar, de tu acercando
florecer.

Y si acaso algún día, alguna persona curiosa, llegara
preguntarte.
¿Que si es verdad que existe el amor a primera vista?
Tú diles que sí, diles que yo te lo dije,
Porque a mí me paso, cuando por primera ves
Yo te divise a ti.

Moon

I look to find the moon each night.
It's always quite a tranquil sight.
I twist my torso, rotate my neck,
I strain my eyes and even curve my back way back.

I like to see it, when it's brand new.
It tells me that the cycle is true.
It unveils itself a section at a time
And when it's full… a celestial poem, complete with rhyme.

Lovers

And when Miss Luna opens up to her full platinum state.
She waits invitingly, suspended, for her cosmic mate *Don Sol*.
And there, two heavenly lovers, entwine themselves,
setting off sparking golden, silver rays.
I rejoice, each time, I witness the galactic consummation of
El Sol y La Luna,
As night, gives way to... Day.

Morning Smile

As the squawking, cackling, laughing sound of excited sea gulls during early morning flight stir me, wake me, from my drowsing state, and the day breaking putt, putt, putt, puttttttttttttttttering, cicada pumping sound of docked shrimp boats bulge emptying the fore nights' seeping high, low tide sea water out of their belly`s bins.

Laboring, I open my still heavy eyelids, hazily squinting towards the dawning eastern horizon, framed by bedroom windowpanes. Adjusting my vision into focus, I take in the new twilight, lavender, blue, cresting above the gold, followed by orange-red, followed by yellow then platinum light.

A prodigious yawn, a deep inhale of moist, salty spice early morning sea breeze, a reverberating stretch, rekindling warm blood flows once again through my reposed vessel veins. I sit up on my side of the bed before rising to my feet, turn to look at you lying next to me still sleeping with a serene, peaceful, angelic face. The kind of perfect portrait face renaissance master painters gave us for the ages.

I remain there awhile, still, silent, beholding, awing your beauty; then, just before I rise, I realize God's purposeful intention when he created you. I stand, and a smile becomes my face.

Ashes

When the time arrives, that I shall no longer bed with you
Because the breath of life has left my body…
And my ashen remains be scattered
To mingle with prevailing winds,
Revolving terra, constant rivers
And churning oceans blue.
Know that wherever it may be
That my powdered cinder remnants
Cling to, or drift to; there… a dancing ember
Of your heartening flame shall too, exist forever forged
By the winds of time, bellowing… the living coals of our love.

Silhouette

I close my eyes fading into the starless night,
That presses me into the dark abyss of sadness,
Laboring against the final extinguishing flicker,
Of a once flaring flame now diminishing within me.
As the last faint twitch of light is about to expire
All hope from me; silhouetting against the backdrop
Of my passing life before me. I am able to vaguely
In my hazed, dazed mind distinguish your presence.
I stretch my arm with trembling hand and reach towards you.
We touch; my eyes once closed in darkness, reopen.

Angel

O' yes indeed, yes indeed,
An angel has this sinner freed!

She lives with me, she cares for me,
She's rain that washes, cleanses me.

I go about my tasks each day.
Her gentle breeze does guide my way.

The wind she uses… to steer me clear,
Of any danger that may come near.

She places me high on a hill,
As I, look up, my God I feel.

I, past each day and onto night,
She shows me stars… in darkness there is light.

She dazzles me with Raven hair,
As I glide, caress her skin so fair.

And like the oceans, we both doth churn.
Because love and life both take their turn.

Of course, with me an angel lives.
She gives and gives and gives and gives…

Her goodness does mountains surpass!
And also, lights, the dark abyss.

Risa

I still have that glorious vision of your birth
Imprinted firmly in my memories.
As I daily refresh your arrival
On that warm, sunny, afternoon in May.
Your mother and I had waited and marked each day of
your term with anxious anticipation.
Your birth became the highlight to our coupled marriage.

The moment my eyes witnessed your puffy-pink-rosy
profile,
Angelically sleeping, nestled comfortably, pure and
wrapped in the warmth
Of newborn cloth. I saw the epiphany of your ancestor's
revolving presence,
Reincarnating, back through you, and yet you were only an
infant, moments old.

Its` hard to imagine, that such a small physical being,
Possess such cosmic power,
Such grandiose ability to reincarnate human traits and
qualities once belonging,
To your grandmother, grandfather, great grandmother,
great grandfather….
That, as long as you shall live, they too shall live, traveling
with creation into infinity…

I remember and shall never forget, holding you for the first
time.
I remember feeling your energy, transmitting dipole
impulses of electricity,
Amplifying my feeling of fatherhood…
Right there and then, I was transformed and catapulted,
into
My next stage in life.

Parenthood!!

A sudden realization of paternal worth holistically encompassed my existence…
As you, a sacred mission, was placed soft and cuddly onto my young father`s arms, creating
An extension to my life that changed entirely, the way I traveled from that day forth.

Mari

Her tawny hair, curled, in cinnamon tresses,
Flaring long, as long as a new day breaking sun ray.
With kindred spirit, she warms the hearts of all she traverses
She is the God made imagery incarnate of a symphonic ballet.

Marisa's Song

The voice! The voice! My Marisa's lovely singing voice!
She was a mere child, my little girl, when first I heard her singing voice.

It was the "Twinkle, Twinkle Little Star" and Jiminy Cricket's "Wish Upon a Star"
Songs she sang; in perfect harmony with the night; my little superstar.

As she gazed in wonder at a Van Gogh starry starry night.
And still today, my memory of her sweet, gifted voice brings me much delight.

And a yearning to hear her sing in tone with the nature that surrounds,
Her musical aura that cosmically abounds, expounds!

Angelina

I see a newborn babe, and what do I see?
I see my Gia Angelina, looking back at me.

I look at her mother Risa E. and what do I see?
I see my Gia, my Angelina, looking back at me.

I turn to look for my wife, my Rita, my Catalina, and what do I see?
I see my Risa, my Gia, and our Angelina Eulogia, looking back at me.

I went to the chapel, to kneel and to pray. My holy rosary, I carry with me…
I close my eyes; pray five sacred mysteries, then when I finish, what do I see?

I see Saint Joseph holding a baby, the both of them smiling, looking right at me.

Carisa Che

My memories are fulfilled now.

If I cannot recall anything else,
From now and till the end of time…
That's good enough for me.

Because your face… your lovely face!
Your make the world go around, beauty face!

Imprints itself, way deep inside of me,
And every day, I live to see,
Your shining face enchanting me.

And thus, your name… Carisa Che,
The child with the pretty face.

It's true my sweet, it's very clear,
Your grace enhances the whole, of humankind.

And so… my memories daily recall with much fondness.
The lovely girl, the possessor of endless jet black, curling hair,
Reaching up to me with boundless affection,

Talking to me, with diamond Che, ebony eyes,
Asking questions… asking why… why and how; do birds fly high.
Who paints the baby blue in sky, why daddy, tell me why?

I answered back as best as I could.
All your questions, all your whys?

And every answer, I gave to you,
Your accepting smile, said back to me.
He must be right; it must be true.

I must say something; I shall always recall.

That yesterday, as today, until forever… way beyond,
When we promised each other with our bonding pledge,
That we would look for… look to… look after… care after…
One another for the rest of our bonded lives.

I`m happy and also very glad
That you became my dearest Che
And I became your dad
My pretty baby, Carisa Che

Remember, when… you took my hand
As we walked the rodeo fair grounds
As I recall you were four back than

As I do mine… you asked me once
To tell you stories

Where is my Child, my little girl?

The time has passed and left me by,
Sitting alone, pensive, praying to angels in the sky.
Asking them to spread their wings wide and fly.
Please swoop to earth, please shade my once little girl
She's left, she's gone, and I remain here old and frail.
My hands now tremble weak and uncertain.
My feet shuffle me about the house in worn out slippers,
I am no longer able to venture outside to clip the rose bush with clippers

I wait all day near the telephone, dozing, waiting for her to call.
The day passes, so too the night, the morrow follows still no call.
She must be busy, preoccupied, making her own way, living her own life.
Still, I lift the phone receiver and place it to my hard of hearing ear.
Maybe, she did call? Perhaps I fell asleep, and her ring I did not hear.
The days give way to nights, the nights to weeks, weeks to months…years.
Alas! at last! A faint distant ringing I think I hear. It must be her, it must be her calling!
My arms, my hands, they fail me, I cannot reach to pick up, she`s calling!

Michael! Gabriel! Rafael! Please! Wait! Wait!
Allow me just one more moment! A moment!
It may be her? She might be calling? She might be calling?
She mi… ght b…. e ca…

Destino

Se acerca ya el crepúsculo de mi buena vida.
Casi tranquilino, y sereno asido mi camino.
Porque, por motivos de la sobrevivencia,
Supero las fallas experiencias de mi pasado.
Prefiriendo mejor, mil veces reflejar sobre
Nuestro bendito destino, ungiro por la gracia
De Dios.

Holy Thursday

I saw a mother crying today.
I had never seen her face before,
But the sound of her pain and sorrow
Echoed in my memories and shook my body to the core.
I couldn't take a steady step. I trembled through my body whole
As I vainly struggled, to distance myself from such
emitting sound… profound, confound, confound in me.

I clasp my ears with hands so tight; I squeeze my head,
grip and pull my hair, in so much anguished agony…
To hear the clawing, clawing, clawing, and wailing sound
that digs such depths inside my Calvary mind.
A weeping mother is what I hear. And me a man, so brave, so brave, so knave
Do engulf myself, with so much fear. To see the origin of my life
My mother, my sister, my mate, my daughter, my wife,
Pronounce disturbance and personal strife.

Bright Eyes

It was a black and starless night, where children covered from the fright
There was no glimmer there was no light, grown men stumbled blind from sight.

The world yielded murderers
For life to steal,
Searching for a man-child with orders to kill.
Imposter kings with harem queens
Feasting on their banquet meals.

The night froze cold, seamless dense; it lasted centuries dulling the memories.
False prophets, with their invented mythological gods, formed a barrier between us and true God.

The world continued its course with moons, unwavering tides and the constant marching of time,
And too the sun, the wind, the stars, persistently, faithfully nurturing, his yet to be bright shining eyes.

The oceans pure, the rain that cleans,
The trees that give us life to breathe.
Green grass by rivers banks,
White covered Mountain tops
And miles and miles of golden crops.

The child, now man, the son of God, our teacher, brother, bright star, guiding light!
He pulled away the black curtain of our abyss. He opened the heavens to eternal bliss.

He showed us the purpose to be, his eyes, his mind, his heart, his soul, our life.

Private Man Prayer

The years have come, and long since gone,
Four daughters fair and tender so,
Have the breath of love upon us blown.
Thus, a greater blessing, I, shall never know.
To see them grow and how God blessed me so.

Reflecting, privately, during alone pensive time, I
sometimes shed a tear.
For it is not a common sight, for a man to publicly weep.
Nor, let it be said, that he is weak and trembles with fear.
So, late at night, when wife and children sleep.
I, look to you up in the skies and wipe the wetness from
my eyes,

I, pray to God, with much redemption, asking still.
That he please grant, on to them good health and wisdom.
And on to me, sensitive emotions, that I may feel.
The need to pray, the need to kneel, and when my time
On earth is done, permission to enter his Kingdom, because
of his Son.

About the Author

Rudy H. Garcia resides with his wife Rita in Laguna Vista, Texas. They are blessed with four lovely daughters and seven beautiful grandchildren. In his first published book, *Life Renewed*, Rudy expresses their romance and his love for family and his faith. Born and raised in the Laguna Madre community, Rudy spent much of his childhood exploring the shores of the Laguna Madre, walking the length of the shrimp docks, venturing in and out of shrimp houses, boarding shrimp boats and conversing with the crew. When he was old enough to work on board a shrimp boat his father sent him to experience the sea ventures with his Uncle Joe and his cousin Eddie.

One of the most treasured memories growing up by the Laguna Madre, was climbing the Port Isabel Lighthouse during the hot summer months. The lighthouse keeper would let Rudy climb the spiral steps to the dome, where he would sit outside on the catwalk overlooking the bay and Padre Island. The East side of the lighthouse's dome provides a cool shade, during the always prevalent sea breeze coming off the Laguna Madre.

Growing up in an area where two countries meet and are only divided by the Rio Grande River, a person acculturates and appreciates the best of two cultures that blend a variety of music, foods, customs, traditions and ceremonies.

The Laguna Madre, Padre Island, Gulf of Mexico and shrimp boats are found in Rudy's literary works. Although Rudy loves writing, he feels he is an educator by vocation and a poet on occasion. His writings stir the awareness and compassion of the hard-working people in South Texas.

www.ingramcontent.com/pod-product-compliance
Lightning Source LLC
Chambersburg PA
CBHW051130160426
43195CB00014B/2410